# Contents

I am a paramedic                        4

Signing in                              6

Checking the equipment                  8

Emergency call                         10

A broken leg                           12

Asthma attack                          14

Standby                                16

Road traffic accident                  18

New baby                               20

Signing off                            22

Glossary                               23

Index                                  24

# I am a paramedic

My name is Candice.

I am a **paramedic**.

I work for
the Shropshire
Ambulance Service
in Craven Arms.

4

# PARAMEDIC

**Rebecca Hunter**

**Photography by
Chris Fairclough**

CHERRYTREE BOOKS

A Cherrytree book

First published in 2006 by
Evans Brothers Ltd
2A Portman Mansions
Chiltern Street
London W1U 6NR

© Evans Brothers Ltd 2006

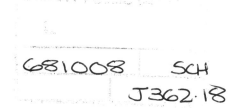

British Library Cataloguing in Publication Data
Hunter, Rebecca
  Paramedic. - (People who help us)
  1. Physicians - Juvenile literature
  I. Title
  610. 6'95

ISBN 1-842-34385-8
13-digit ISBN (from 1 Jan 2007) 978-1-842-34385-2

Planned and produced by Discovery Books Ltd
Editor: Rebecca Hunter
Designer: Ian Winton

**Acknowledgements**
Commissioned photography by Chris Fairclough.

The author, packager and publisher would like to thank Candice Roe, Malcolm Saunders, the staff at Craven Arms Ambulance Station, Daphne Lewis and Shropshire and West Midland Ambulance Service NHS Trust for their participation in this book.

Words appearing in bold like this, are explained in the glossary.

Today I am on a day **shift**. I arrive at the ambulance **base station** at seven o'clock in the morning.

Malcolm is an ambulance **technician**. I will be working with him today.

# Signing in

Inside the crew room I say hello to Dave. He is just finishing the night shift. It is nearly time for him to go home.

I write my name on the signing-in sheet. This shows what time I started work.

Then I go to the kitchen to make some tea.

# Checking the equipment

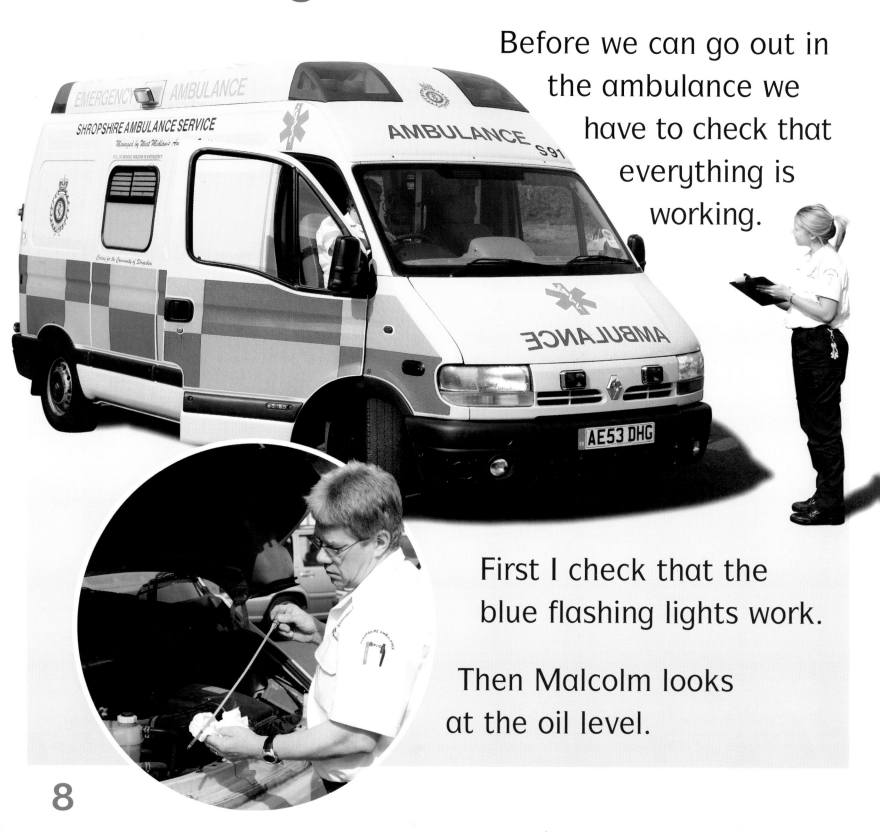

Before we can go out in the ambulance we have to check that everything is working.

First I check that the blue flashing lights work.

Then Malcolm looks at the oil level.

8

Inside the ambulance I check that the medical bag has a complete set of supplies.

This machine is a defibrillator. It is used to restart someone's heart after a **heart attack**. I print out a sheet of paper to check it is working.

# Emergency call

The phone rings. It is Control, the place where the 999 **emergency** calls are first received. I write down the address of where we have to go.

I run to the ambulance. Malcolm is waiting for me.

We leave the ambulance station with our blue lights flashing and the **siren** sounding.

We are on our way to help somebody in trouble.

# A broken leg

We arrive at a building site. A new house is being built there. A builder has just fallen off the roof.

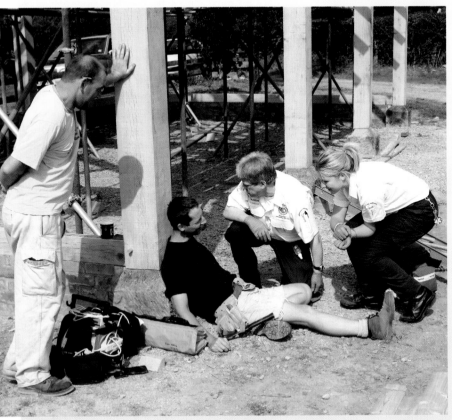

He says his leg really hurts. I think he has broken it.

We strap his leg into a **splint** to keep it still. We also give him some **oxygen** through a mask.

We put him on a stretcher and move him into the ambulance.

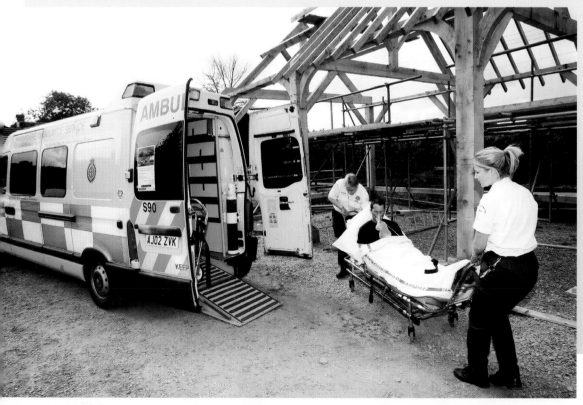

We will take him to hospital where they will put his leg in a plaster cast.

13

# Asthma attack

Our next patient is a little boy called Joe. He is having an **asthma** attack. This means he can't breathe properly.

I give him a mask and some **oxygen**. Malcolm carries him to the ambulance.

In the ambulance I check Joe's mask. I give him some ventolin, which will help open up his airways.

On the way to the hospital I have to fill in a patient report form. I ask Joe's mother some questions about his health.

# Standby

Control rings and tells us to go into town on standby. We will wait here until we get another **emergency** call.

It is lunchtime now, so Malcolm and I get a sandwich.

People often come and talk to us when we are on standby.

Somebody tells us that an elderly man has fainted and fallen over.

He is not injured, but he cannot get up by himself.

We help him to his feet and he says he feels well enough to go home.

# Road traffic accident

I get a call on the radio. There has been a road traffic accident nearby.

At road accidents we have to wear **protective** clothing. I put on my yellow jacket, helmet and blue gloves.

The young driver is **unconscious**. We put a collar around his neck so we won't hurt him when we remove him from the car.

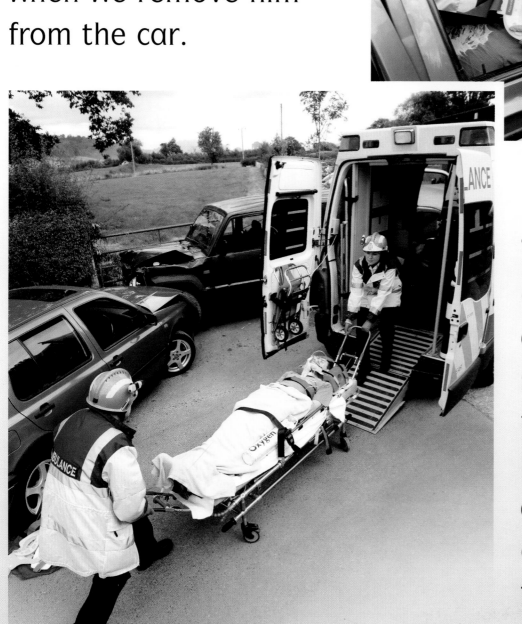

Then we put him on a **spinal board** and strap him up securely. We will take him to A and E, the accident and emergency department at the hospital.

# New baby

Our last call today is to a pregnant woman. Lindsay is about to have a baby. She needs to get to hospital quickly. We strap her into a carry chair and take her to the ambulance.

I check her **blood pressure** and give her some **gas and air** from a mask. This will help her **labour pains**.

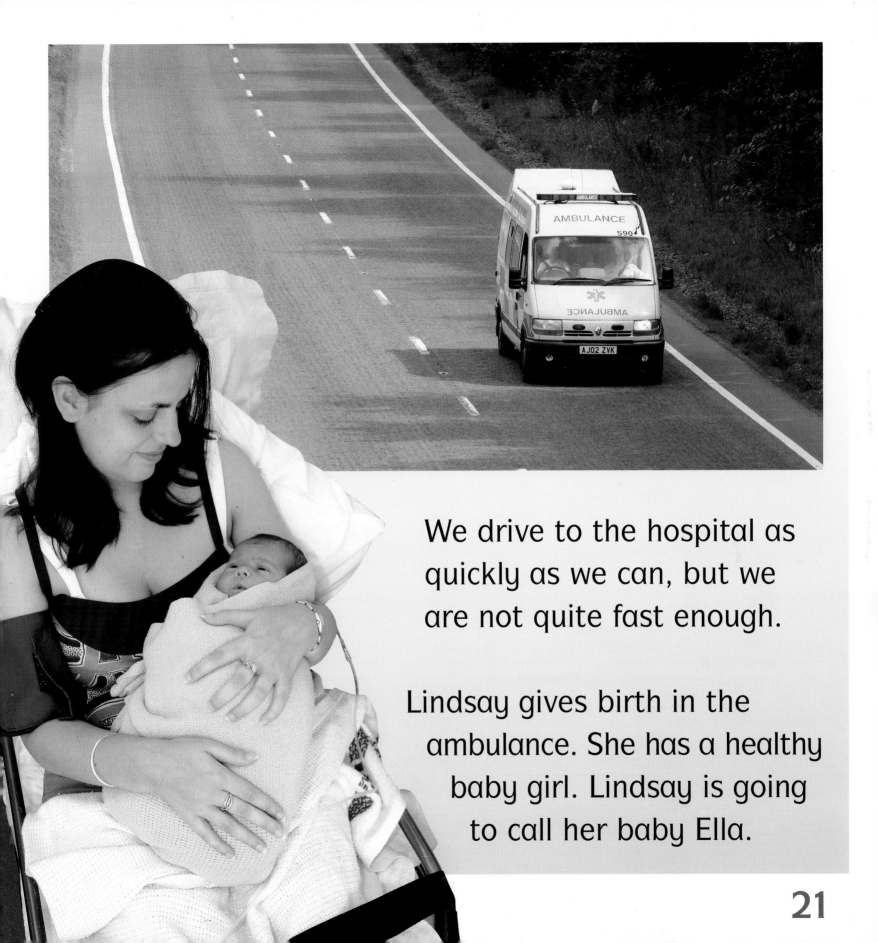

We drive to the hospital as quickly as we can, but we are not quite fast enough.

Lindsay gives birth in the ambulance. She has a healthy baby girl. Lindsay is going to call her baby Ella.

# Signing off

When we get back to the **base station** I go to the store cupboard. I check the supplies.

It is nearly seven o'clock and the end of my **shift**. The night shift have arrived. After a long and busy day it is now time for me to go home.

# Glossary

**asthma** a disease of the chest that causes wheezing and makes it hard to breathe

**base station** the place where the ambulance crew is based

**blood pressure** a measurement that shows how well your blood is flowing through your body

**crew room** the living room at the base station where the paramedics can sit, have coffee, read books or watch television

**emergency** a serious situation that must be dealt with immediately

**gas and air** special mixture of a medical gas and air to help the pain go away

**heart attack** a serious medical condition that causes the heart to stop beating

**labour pains** the pains a woman has when she is having a baby

**oxygen** the gas that we need to breathe

**paramedic** a highly qualified emergency care worker

**protective** preventing something or someone from being hurt

**shift** a set period during which people work

**siren** the howling noise that an ambulance, police car or fire engine makes

**spinal board** a board that an injured person is strapped to after an accident

**splint** a straight piece of equipment that is tied to a broken arm or leg to stop it moving

**technician** a qualified emergency care worker

**unconscious** in a state similar to sleep, as a result of an accident or injury

# Index

ambulance  8, 9, 10, 11, 13, 15, 19, 20, 21

ambulance technician  5

asthma  14, 15

baby  20, 21

base station  5

birth  20, 21

blood pressure  20

broken leg  12, 13

car accident  18, 19

carry chair  20

defibrillator  9

emergency calls  10, 16, 18

equipment  8, 9

gas and air  20

heart attack  9

labour pains  20

lights  8, 11

lunch  16

medical bag  9, 14, 17

neck collar  19

oil  8

oxygen  13, 14

patient report form  15

protective clothing  18, 19

road traffic accident  18, 19

shifts  5, 6, 22

signing in  7, 8

siren  11

spinal board  19

splint  13

standby  16

store cupboard  22

stretcher  13

supplies  9, 22